The Zen of Running

The Zen of Running

Fred Rohé

Photography by Dennis Anderson

Calligraphy by Paul Tescher

A Random House-Bookworks Book

Seventh printing, March 1978

Photographs by Dennis Anderson
Calligraphy by Paul Tescher
Solar Light by Bob Stricker
Prana by Rubin Glickman
Printed and bound under the supervision of
Dean Ragland, Random House

This book is co-published by   Random House Inc.
                                 201 East 50th Street
                                 New York, N.Y. 10022

                           and   The Bookworks
                                 628 Vincente Ave.
                                 Berkeley, Ca. 94707

Distributed in the United States by Random House,
and simultaneously published in Canada
by Random House of Canada Limited, Toronto.
Booksellers please order from Random House.

Rohé, Fred
     The Zen of Running
       1. Jogging. I. Title
GV494.R56   128'.2   74-20924
ISBN 0-394-49611-6
ISBN 0-394-73038-0 pbk.

Manufactured in the United States of America

dedicated to
Paul Reps, my spiritual father,
Paul Hawken, my spiritual brother and running mate
and Sandy, my wife, lover, closest friend.

In the winter of 1969, after about nine months of regular running, I was visiting my friend Reps, a writer of poetic books about wholly living (*Zen Flesh, Zen Bones, Ten Ways to Meditate, New Uses of the Human Instrument*).

"Maybe I should write a book about running," I said.

"Maybe you should wait," he said.

"O.K., I haven't earned the right to write such a book yet. I should wait about three years."

But I didn't. I wrote the first version that afternoon, there on the island of Hawaii, standing in front of Reps' window looking down the mountain across green fields of sugarcane to the blue Pacific, using the window sill for a table.

It's now the autumn of 1973 and I've been a regular runner for more than four years. The book has been expanded by several short, intense, creative bursts following particularly inspiring jaunts on my favorite running track, the ocean beach of San Francisco. It feels like I've earned the right to present *The Zen of Running*. It truly expresses the joy of running.

This experience is
a newly discovered
form of meditation
or
one more way
for you
to discover you.
so I suggest you
joyfully,
exuberantly,
take a short run.
(short might be
10 yards or 10 blocks –
that's your own
private affair.)

do your run in the cleanest air you can find.
be as undressed as possible so that you get
well bathed by sun and air.

if there's a beach or a park without a lot of broken glass, do your run barefoot. this gives you a foot massage which stimulates all the nerve reflex points in the soles of your feet, which in turn stimulate all the organs of your body. by being barefoot you also get grounded, this direct contact with Great Mother Earth meaning that electrical equilibrium is established between you and the planet.

in this dance of joy
which is your run
breathe in long
thru your nose
breathe out short and sharp
thru your mouth.

there might be 4 steps
to the in-breath
with the out-breath
on the fifth step,
the point of counting
being RHYTHM —
maybe not 4/1 but 2/1 or 5/3 —
YOUR rhythm.

(on the other hand
you may find
that breathing out thru the nose
works better for you
than breathing out thru the mouth.
if so, of course do it your way.
nobody but you
should tell you what to do.)

at first you may pant sharply
in and out with every step.
so what?
run a little more,
dancingly, joyfully,
loving this gift we've all been given
and *little by little*
as your run lengthens
your breath will lengthen.

don't overdo it.
underdo it.
you aren't running because
you're in a hurry to get somewhere

you will be able to run tirelessly
if you follow this simple rule:
Run *within* your breath,
do not run *ahead* of your breath.
(you have to run
to discover what that means.)

every time you run
you create the quality
of your own experience.

runners often speak of pain
and of course if you want that
you can have all you want
merely by pushing yourself
beyond your limits
every time you run.

it's your choice of whether
to run to *punish* your self
or to *experience* your self.
if you choose, with me, the latter,
then every run can be joyful
the key words are,
Take it easy!
create your self as a runner
gradually, patiently, relaxedly.

you can be victimized
by your imagination
if you imagine yourself
astonishing your world
with your progress and prowess.
we know this mechanism as Ego,
we know this state as Ambition.

being Great Runners
is not the attainment we need.
it is self control.
without it, ego forces us into ambition
and the price of ambition
is pain.

let's not be egotistical,
let's take it easy.

your creation of you
as a runner
will be a pleasure
as you progress
by running *less*

the key to the "progress by less" method
is always to do
less than you think you can.

if you think you can gallop right away,
just take a walk.

thinking you can run around the block,
just run down to the corner.

you have the rest of your life
to progress into long distance running.
why strain, make pain?
why not lope along,
free and easy,
doing it like a dance?
when you start doing it
you'll see that running
is naturally hard enough
all by itself
without you creating
additional hardship for yourself.

so, practically speaking,
you might ask,
How far should I run?
and I would answer
by saying
you must answer that for you.

you see,
it's quite a relative and individual thing,
this distance question.
how old are you?
how long are your legs?
how much do you weigh?
what imaginary distance
do you feel comfortable with?

since individual idiosyncracies
make it impossible to generalize safely
about distance
it's really a matter of *time*.
how far do your legs
take you in, say,
five or fifty minutes?
you should run far enough
to make yourself feel dandy
and if you don't
you've probably run
too far.

you might ask
How fast should I run?

speed, too, is relative
to a lot of individual considerations:
      maybe you're short and heavy
      maybe you're long and lean
      maybe you haven't given up smoking yet
      maybe you want real bad to be *fast*,
      maybe you couldn't care less about that --

you should run fast enough
to make yourself breathe hard
and sweat freely.
if you're running fast enough
to make yourself pant and sweat
you're running fast enough.

(but of course
you are living
your life.
so if you want
to run against the clock
remember that this is *your* game --
you decide what rules
you want to play by.)

you might ask
How often should I run?

the objective is to build strength and endurance
to the point of being able to run effortlessly,
compared to the capability you experienced when
you took your first run.

so run often enough,
whether daily or four times a week,
to increase and maintain
strength and endurance
but not often enough
to turn it
into drudgery.

after a while
running regularly
will feel so much better
than not
that you will just naturally
run regularly
according to what feels good
to you
and that will be
often enough.

people ask me
What should a runner eat?

if you don't know
what you should eat
then neither do I.
if I thought I did
I would do you a favor
by not telling you,
allowing you the independent adventure
of discovering for you
how to feed you.

your food should help you
feel light, clean, clear and strong.
so I recommend
the simple principles I call
the XYZ of eating:
X~ eat pure, whole foods
Y~ eat simply, according to appetite
Z~ eat slowly, gratefully, joyfully.

altho you shouldn't let anyone
tell you *how* to run,
any more than you should let anyone
tell you how to run
your life,
there is one principle
useful to all who run:
Run as *erect* as possible!

seen from the side,
your spine should be exactly vertical to the ground;
if you lean forward while running,
you hang the weight of your torso
out over your lifting legs,
your forward leg acting like a brace
to keep you from falling on your face,
making it harder to lift your leg
for the next stride
and slowing you, tiring you.

running erectly --
shoulders, chest,
abdomen, hips,
in one plumb line --
your legs lift easily,
knees thrusting up
and forward
freely.

the troubles with the other books
I've seen about running
are two:
1. they have a mechanical approach,
   telling us how far to run
   how often, how fast
   as if we are all the same,
   like a fleet of two-door sedans
and 2. by making it
   a mechanical practice
   the spirit is missing --
   there is no *fun!*

my friend Reps says
"unless it's fun
better left undone."

remember: we create our world(s)
with our mind(s).
so let your mind say
"look, I'm running
and all runners do this beautiful dance, each
stride a leap thru space -- ho! what fun!"

once you've discovered
running is just another
form of funning
you will establish
your running speed,
time, distance and regularity
according to what
is right for you.

becoming a regular runner
means certain rewards
begin to accrue to physical you.

- heart pump-muscle strengthens, slowing pulse,
  increasing longevity potential.

- lung resiliency and capacity increase, nasal
  passages blow clean.

- equilibrium between intake and outgo is established,
  proper natural body weight is maintained.

- feet and legs become strong and firm.

- skin and eyes sparkle with vitality.

    but if the dance of the run
    isn't fun
    then discover another dance
    because without fun
    the good of the run
    is undone
    and a suffering runner
    always quits
    sooner or later.

you will find your dancing run
doesn't tire you but *energizes you.*

grossly: as your muscles strengthen, your lungs
expand and your circulation goes quicker, deeper.
thus your oxygenation from in-breathing and your
expulsion of toxins from out-breathing becomes more
thorough, more complete. also, your strongly, sharply
moving abdominal muscles massage your intestines
into action while the opening of your pores to the
flow of sweat completes the cleansing.

and subtly: by running within your breath, you store
a surplus of "prana", a Sanscrit word meaning
Absolute Energy, the invisible vital force which
supplies the primal motivation for every form of
activity.

you may want to run
with a friend or a loved one
but running is not ecstatic
unless it is graced
by your own natural pace.

with a running mate
whose pace matches yours,
you can run side by side
stride by stride
feet slapping ground as one
two breathing as one
dancing the oneness
of human being.

you can run away
from all your troubles
as your run gets right.

I took it slowly
easily making my run longer
little by little getting stronger
until one day I felt so free
it no longer seemed to be me
but rather he
and he had earned this strength
that feels like lightness
and turned his short run
into a long one
then turned his long run
into the rightness
of this dancing ---

experiencing the run as dance
requires some special attention.

be aware of your head —
it should float on your neck.
(fix your gaze on an object;
it will stay level, not bounce up and down.)

your neck should be loose,
your shoulders should hang easy.

notice your arms —
their swing should be close to your side,
they don't need tightly clenched fists,
just loosely, comfortably closed.

feel your feet —
heel, toes, heel, toes,
the heel cushioning your return to earth,
the toes vaulting you off again.

being aware of the details
of your running
gives you economy of energy
leading to purity of movement —
running free and easy,
loping loosely and lightly — *dancing!*

as you become strong
you gain spring in your stride.
there will be days
when your dancing
even feels like flying
because, look, it *is* flying --
between each springing stride
you float for an instant
free in the air
before you touch down
for the next springing up,
leaping forward stride.

please remember that the point of your running
is to help you become
healthy, happy and wholly you.
consider also accompanying
your breath with
a prayer (like 'God's Grace')
or a mantra (like 'Om')
or a feeling (like 'Love')
or a question (like 'Who am I?')
or whatever you like --
it's a private affair --
breathing it in and out
to your own private running rhythm
(for remember, this is *your* discovery).

what do I mean calling this running
"a newly discovered form of meditation?"
Isn't meditation done sitting cross-legged
on the floor with closed eyes?

I mean that meditation is a state of being,
not a physical position.
I can run in a state that is just as meditative,
perhaps more so,
than when sitting Buddha-like.

from the experience of running meditatively,
I learn that potentially my entire life
can be lived meditatively.
and it seems to me I should learn to live it so.
to me this means that I will be
calmly, courageously, alertly, intelligently, energetically
present for each moment of my living
until life is done with this body.

so one aspect of running meditation
is the sheer joy right now of this running.
another aspect
is the learning process
which uses this running as a metaphor
for all the rest of my life.

whatever you do
with your running,
you only cheat yourself
by pushing, pressing, competing.

there are no standards
and no possible victories except
the joy you are living
while dancing your run.
in any life
joy is only known
in this moment --now!

so feel the flow
of your dance
and know
you are not running
for some future reward --
the real reward is *now!*
                    in the running
                    in the run
                    --- now ---
                    why not start
                    now?

just before beginning to write this line,
I took my pulse.
my heart beat 48 times in one minute.
I observe this body I live in
and see that it is lean and strong,
the eyes are clear, the skin glows.
the running is obviously a wonderful tonic
for this body.
and what is good for the body
is good for the whole man.
our spirit is not separate from our body
any more than the water is separate from the stream.
the water *is* the stream.

a certain lady whom I love,
and for whom I have an immense amount of respect,
read what I have written
and said that it is beautiful.
but, she said, there is something missing.
do you really mean, she asked,
that it is always joyful, always fun?
no, it is not.
what do I do when I don't feel like running,
when I feel more like just lying around?
sometimes I do that, I just lie around.
and see that about myself.
but then, sometimes I push myself out there to run
even tho the predominant feeling is,
I don't want to.
and see that about myself.
because there is more than one side
to this group I call "myself".
there is no single, permanent "I"
but rather there are many.
one "I" wants to run,
several miles later
another "I" wants to quit.
usually I keep on running
because it's a faster way to get back
to where I started from. anyway, the "I" that
wanted to run will appear again soon.

in speaking of my self, I say "I" or "me"
or "myself", obscuring the fact that I am
not one but many.
there is a truly significant side of "me" that
loves to run, but I have *not* run for weeks at a
time, said yes to other sides.
        my aim in life is not to run
        but to awaken.
        CONSCIOUSNESS requires SEEING
        begins with opening to what you are.

sure people are lazy.
me too.
I try hard
to see myself clearly
and clear as can be
there's the lazy side of me.
most often, then,
I simply choose not
to feed the lazy side of me.
the device I use to get around him
is discipline.
discipline is one more aspect
of our running yoga.
(yes, it's a yoga too,
and yoga always requires discipline.)

but the lazy side of you
is not exactly the same as
the lazy side of me.
so your discipline
is your responsibility to invent
don't be afraid of it,
discipline is good for us too.

all that I wrote about running is my truth,
is from an important side of my self,
came from the desire to give of my self.
running is not all ecstasy, all positive.
sometimes running is suffering intentionally
for the sake of seeing, sometimes running is
resisting and suffering *unintentionally* because
we are human beings.
let's not make our running a fantasy,
let's let our running be real.

I sit here recalling a run of a few days ago,
I remember that I wanted to capture this
essence with these words ~~~
    I am running
    free and easy,
    my breath rolling in,
    pouring out,
    entirely present
    in the now of this experience,
       mind
          still.

as I run
I can feel my face
beaming ecstatically.

so may you.

if you like,
drop me a line
telling me
what's true for you.